The Everyday Life Bible: Notes & Commentary by Joyce Meyer. First Edition: Faith
Words. New York, NY 2020. Print.
https://www.youversion.com/apps/New International Version
https://www.youversion.com/apps/New King James Version
https://www.youversion.com/apps/King James Version
https://www.youversion.com/apps/Message Version

LWI Publishing Services

Contact info:
info@joanldavislifecoaching.com
www.joanldavislifecoaching.com

Printed in the United States of America
First Printing: March 2023

≫ Table of Contents

>> Table of Contents

FEAR NOT, MY CHILD

Life experiences can sometimes make you feel too inadequate to accept the call God is sending to you. This is especially true when you look at all that has happened in your life, and when the weight of life has consumed and caused you to feel discouraged. So, you say to yourself, "How can God be calling me, knowing where I have come from, where I have been, and what I have done? What would the Lord possibly want with me?" But I can remember the Lord saying to me, "Fear not, my child, for all things are working together for your good. I will be with you always. I will carry you into those places that have been predestined a long time ago, and no weight of life will hinder my plans for your life. So again I say, fear not, my child."

I was truly amazed at what the Lord had spoken, which took my breath away. But even with God's reassurance, I could not help but to question at times. "Why me, God? How can I, God? Why is it so difficult for me to surrender to Your voice, God? Why am I allowing my life experiences, the weight of it all, to consume so much of my life? Why am I allowing it to make me feel that I am not qualified to be called by God? Why am I feeling so unworthy to be amongst the elected and proclaim the Good News of Jesus Christ?" I know that I am not the only one who has asked these questions and felt this way. I feel so afraid, but God will not stop speaking to me. I am constantly wrestling with God's call for me to surrender to His voice. I am constantly wrestling with feelings of inadequacy. And this is why! From my beginning until now, God has been working His purpose in my life.

I had turned in so many directions, but all my feet could do was stumble and cause me to fall. My reflection in the mirror let me know that I needed something more for my life than I could find on my own. In 2013, I found myself at an evening worship service, sitting with a heart of uncertainty and an empty inner cup, looking for something to fill me up. I needed something to make my days brighter and a bit more hopeful. I was searching for something more. My mind was consumed with so much, but secretly longing desperately for something supernatural to happen to me that would turn my sadness to happier days. I heard an invitation being made by the pastor of the church. I can still hear her voice like it was yesterday. She said, "If you know God is calling you to ministry, come up, and He will do the rest."

Just thinking about this moment, I am taken back to when God says to the Prophet Jeremiah, "Before I formed thee in the belly, I knew thee; and before thou camest forth out of the womb I sanctified thee, and I ordained thee a prophet unto the nations." [Jeremiah 1:5 (KJV)] I knew at that moment that I was always in God's plans. He had a plan for my life, and it had been revealed to me. It took some time for me to realize what the plan was, but it was made clear to me that day.

I have come to the realization that no journey is ever an easy one. On the contrary, obeying the voice of God also requires you to fight and to keep believing that the journey you said yes to was meant for you. No sooner had I started my studies, I was faced again, like many others in life, with challenges. I lost my car. My children and I were on the verge of being homeless. I sought more of God's guidance once again. Surely, God did not fail me. In fact, I experienced the faithfulness of God. I had many deep conversations with God, reminding Him of His promises and my obedience to His calling. One morning, after my devotional time with God, I walked out of the door onto my porch and sat, waiting for my ride to class. A dark patch of clouds was forming over my porch. I turned my eyes towards the sky. The dark clouds began to separate, and it was then when I heard the voice of God say, "I just wiped away your dark days." Right then and there, I knew God was up to something greater. My response to Him was, "Thank you, Jesus." From that day forward, I never forgot that God would be with me always. In God's perfect timing, I was blessed with a car. A few days later, my children and I were moving into another house. The rent was less, and the space was comfortable for my family. God reminded me in all of this that He cared for me and that His love was real. He reminded me that I should never forget His word:

> *"Fear thou not, for I am with thee; be not dismayed; for I am thy God:*
> *I will strengthen thee; yea, I will help thee; yea, I will uphold thee*
> *with the right hand of my righteousness."*
> *-Isaiah 41:10 (KJV)*

Looking back on all that I have had to experience in my life, I genuinely believe our challenges and obstacles do not take away the fact that God promises to take care of us. Although my challenges were overwhelming, God always showed up and kept His promises to me. And He continuously does what He promised in my life.

To fully understand what it truly means to Surrender to the Voice of God, in my own obedience I accept the charge in writing this workbook. The purpose of this "Surrendering to the Voice of God Workbook" is to help and guide you into a deeper commitment to the Voice of God.

So, to all who will read this book, I pray it will help you understand and allow God to direct and speak to you on your journey in surrendering.

Chapter 1

HEARING THE VOICE OF GOD

He that hath ears to hear, let him hear.
Matthew 11:15

The Gospel according to Matthew 11:15 says; "He that hath ears to hear, let him hear." Let us exegesis this verse so that we can fully embrace and understand our journey in hearing the voice of God. The Word says "He that hath ears to hear." Matthew was not only speaking to hearing what is happening around our surroundings, but rather to be attentive to hearing what God is speaking to us. The way our world, our societies, and our communities are right now, it is so easy to hear everything else around us, and not only hear everything but also get caught up in the happenings and not be in tune to hearing the Voice of God. The second half of the verse says; "let him hear." Letting us know God want to have communications with us. He wants us to take time out of our busy lives and sit with Him. Sitting with Him will allow our Heavenly Father to love, comfort, and guide us in hearing His Voice.

Matthew was clear in this verse; "He that hath ears to hear, let him hear." Teaching us to draw closer to the One who cares, but not only cares, the One who knows the plans for us. The One who is the Creator, the One who loves us so much that He created us in His own image.

As you consider ways to draw closer to Him and hear the voice of God, consider meditation, where you enter into quiet time with the Father and allow the Holy Spirit to prepare you so that you can hear the Voice of God.

Now as we prepare to enter into our meditation, we have our guidelines we follow that will help us getting into our time of quietness.

Here are some items you can use:

- **Find a quiet location**
- **Your bible**
- **Surrendering to the voice of God book**
- **Surrendering to the voice of God workbook where you can journal what you hear**
- **Soothing sounds (waterfalls, instrumentals, etc.)**
- **Be sure you put your phone on DND so you are not disturbed - this time is for you and your Heavenly Father**
- **Once settle, take a few deep breaths**

If you are not used to meditating, it may feel a little awkward in the beginning but as you do it over and over, it will get easier.

Settling in the presence to hear God's Voice can be an incredible experience, you just have to lean in. Jesus teaches us in His own meditation the use of the Word. Having the Word as part of our meditation process help us to draw closer in hearing the Voice of God. The prophet Isaiah, reminds us of how much God promises that He will always be with us. The Word says, "So do not fear, for I am with you; do not be dismayed, for I am your God. I will strengthen you and help you; I will uphold you with my righteous right hand." An amazing word of encouragement to Israel" [Isaiah 41:10 (NIV)]. This is one of my favorite Scriptures in the Bible. As you settle down, I encourage you to read this verse a few times, the second time you read it, read it slower and allow the Words to settle in your soul, when you read the 3rd time, meditate on the word(s) in the scripture that speaks to you. What you are doing in that moment is releasing everything and asking the Holy Spirit to take full control.

Now let us journey into hearing the Voice of God.

Meditation

The prompting of God's voice has a purpose. God is reaching out because He has a purpose for you and He wants to help you work through some things in your life so you can reach the fullness of what has been predestined for you. He is trying to take you to where He wants to send you to be a blessing, a means of inspiration, a voice of encouragement, and a vessel of strength to help others through their challenges. What God needs is for you to allow Him to remove your doubts and fears. You must surrender everything to Him. These distractions must be removed so that He can position you to hear His voice more clearly. God speaks to us in so many different ways because He shares a language with those He created. He has many ways of speaking directly to us which become clearer as we draw closer to Him and develop our relationship with Him. The language is beautiful, and we are able to identify God's voice separate from all else. He wants us to recognize His voice so that He can use us to speak for Him. For some of us, God speaks through songs, for others by reading a book, and to some He speaks when they are being still in the moment. Whatever way God uses to get our attention, once we hear from Him, He can use us to speak for Him. The Bible tells us how God used the prophets to be His voice to speak to the people. For example, He used Jeremiah to warn the people so they could turn from their wrong ways. Similarly, Jonah was used to warn the people of Nineveh of its coming destruction and Moses was used to free the Israelites from the bondage of slavery with Pharaoh. Whatever means God uses, we must be ready to hear what He is telling us and where He is telling us to go. We have to be free from that which distracts us and makes us feel inadequate to serve. We must be completely turned toward God in order to hear and receive. I pray that you will be in a position to hear from God the plans He has for you.

Reflection

How has it been challenging for you to surrender to God's voice in your life?

_____

_____

_____

_____

_____

Have you been exhausted by the challenges in your life that have made it seem as though God is so far away?

_____

_____

_____

_____

Do you seek God faithfully when you are confronted by life's disappointments?

_____

_____

_____

_____

Have you ever missed hearing the Voice of God because you were so consumed in the happenings? Be honest, list those times, and hear what God is saying to you now.

_____

_____

_____

_____

Scriptures - KJV/NIV/MSG

SCRIPTURE	VERSE		
Psalm 37:5	"Commit thy way unto the Lord; trust also in Him; and He shall bring it to pass."		KJV
Psalm 37:5	"Commit your way to the Lord; trust in him and he will do this:"		NIV
Psalm 37:5	"Open up before God, keep nothing back; he'll do whatever needs to be done;"		MSG
2 Corinthians 12:10	"Therefore I take pleasure in infirmities, in reproaches, in necessities, in persecutions, in distresses for Christ's sake: for when I am weak, then am I strong."		KJV
2 Corinthians 12:10	"That is why, for Christ's sake, I delight in weaknesses, in insults, in hardships, in persecutions, in difficulties. For when I am weak, then I am strong."		NIV
2 Corinthians 12:10	"Now I take limitations in stride, and with good cheer, these limitations that cut me down to size—abuse, accidents, opposition, bad breaks. I just let Christ take over! And so the weaker I get, the stronger I become."		MSG
Isaiah 41:13	"For I the Lord thy God will hold thy right hand, saying unto thee, Fear not; I will help thee."		KJV
Isaiah 41:13	"For I am the Lord your God who takes hold of your right hand and says to you, Do not fear; I will help you."		NIV
Isaiah 41:13	"Because I, your God, have a firm grip on you and I'm not letting go. I'm telling you, 'Don't panic. I'm right here to help you."		MSG
John 16:13	"Howbeit when He, the Spirit of truth, is come, He will guide you into all truth: for He shall not speak of himself; but whatsoever he shall hear, that shall He speak: and He will shew you things to come."		KJV
John 16:13	"But when he, the Spirit of truth, comes, he will guide you into all the truth. He will not speak on his own; he will speak only what he hears, and he will tell you what is yet to come."		NIV
John 16:13	"But when the Friend comes, the Spirit of the Truth, he will take you by the hand and guide you into all the truth there is. He won't draw attention to himself, but will make sense out of what is about to happen and, indeed, out of all that I have done and said."		MSG

Prayer

Heavenly Father, I come to You, thanking You for the things You have and continue to do for me. Lord Jesus, I ask You to teach me what it means to surrender to Your voice. Being obedient to Your voice, answering Your ways, committing to Your will, is all I desire. Father, I seek You more. Help me to know more about what it means to trust in You. Help me do what You ask of me, rather than fearing the unknown. Holy Spirit, I invite You to take full control and guide me into the presence in hearing The Father's Voice. Help me learn what it means to be open to Your will so that You can be glorified through me, Father. Let the words of my mouth and the meditations of my heart be acceptable in Your sight. I pray this prayer believing it is done, in Jesus' name. Amen, amen, and amen.

Now I invite you to write your own personal covenant prayer with God, In Hearing His Voice.

Personal Prayer

Heavenly Father,

Chapter 2

RESISTING THE VOICE OF GOD

Behold, I stand at the door, and knock: if any man hear my voice, and open the door, I will come in to him, and will sup with him, and he with me.
Revelation 3:20

The Book of Revelation tells of the Second Coming of Our Lord and Savior. The book provides a full explanation on all the fulfillments in detail of what will happen when we are resistant to the Voice of God. Because the Book of Revelation tells of the Second Coming, some preachers do not preach, teach, or explain from this book. Allow me to be bold by saying I strongly disagree with anyone who does not want to preach, teach, or explain this book. No Books in the entire 66 Books of the Bible, should not be preached, taught, or explained from. Why? Each Book provides a guideline into having a personal relationship with The Heavenly Father. I find the Book of Revelation to be a Book of Second Chances, reminding us of the two thieves that were next to Jesus on the Cross, both committed dreadful sins, while one decided to join with the crowd and mock Jesus, the other sought Jesus right there in the midst of his penalty for his sinful act, and Jesus forgave him, reassuring him that he too will be in paradise with Him. The Book of Revelation is like that to me, God is offering at the very end, another chance. Even after reading through the 65 Books prior, some of us still may not understand or get it, but this book, tells us what will happen when we resist His voice, when we live to follow other paths and not the one God set for us, the path His Son Jesus Christ modeled for us. We can find reassurance in Christ, there is hope in the midst of resisting, but why wait until it gets to this point?

That is what we find happening in Chapter 3. Chapter 3 focuses on the warnings to the seven churches. It covers three churches out of the seven, Sardis churches verses 1-3, Philadelphia churches verses 7-13, and the rest of the chapter covers the churches in Laodicea verses 14-22. Revelation 3:20 is teaching us as we prepare for the Second Coming of Our Lord and Savior. It reads, "Behold, I stand at the door, and knock: if any man hear my voice, and open the door, I will come in to him, and will sup with him, and he with me." Let us approach this verse step by step; "Behold, I stand at the door, and knock", this portion of the verse is not referring to a physical door. Our Heavenly Father is such a gentleman while He knows us inside and outside, and knows the plans He has for us, He still doesn't push or force Himself onto us. He approaches us with respect and allows us the opportunity to welcome Him in. We see this in the other part of that verse; "if any man hear my voice, and open the door" look how such a gentleman Our Heavenly Father is to us. The One who is in control is letting us know we have a choice, "if you want Me, by hearing My Voice and not resisting My Voice, and you open the door", look what He says will happen in the rest of the verse. He says, "I will come in to him, and will sup with him, and he with me." Our Heavenly Father wants to have a personal intimate relationship with each of us. Remember now, He created us in His Own image, from the beginning of time, from the foundation of the first Book 1- Genesis, now here we are in the last Book 66 - Revelation and God still wants that personal relationship with us. Through our many sinful acts and disobedience towards Him, He said; "I will come in and sup, to sup means to eat, dine, break bread, and get to know each other on a different level. God wants our moments spent with Him, so that He can pour out all the love that each one of us deserves. To be treated like royalty as Our Father created us to be.

Now as you prepare to meditate, below are some strategies you can follow and some items you will need to help you get into a time and space of quiet stillness.

Here are some items you can use:

- Find a quiet location
- Your bible
- Surrendering to the voice of God book
- Surrendering to the voice of God workbook where you can journal what you hear
- Soothing sounds (waterfalls, instrumentals, etc.)
- Be sure you put your phone on DND so you are not disturbed - this time is for you and your Heavenly Father
- Once settled, take a few deep breaths

If you are not used to meditating, it may feel a little awkward in the beginning but as you do it over and over, it will get easier.

Open yourself to what God has for you, according to David, a man of God's heart who found great favor with Him (with God). David through his own meditation with the Father, sought Him directly to hear, in order not to resist God's Voice. I now invite you to use one of David's psalms in your time of seeking God. Psalm 139:7 "Where can I go from Your Spirit? Where can I flee from Your Presence?" Experiencing this type of spiritual disciplines through God's Word will help us to draw closer to Him. What you are doing is releasing everything and asking the Holy Spirit to take full control.

I invite you to practice one of the many Spiritual Disciplines, "Meditation" as you entered into your quiet time.

Meditation

Having Spiritual Disciplines teaches us to enter into a time where we do not have to be resistant to God's Voice. Meditation is an integral part of your journey in listening to the voice of God. Your meditation time with God should be a time well spent without worrying about what is next. It is a time for you to empty your mind, let everything go and come into the presence of God. You may be saying at this point how is this spiritual discipline going to help you not be resistant to listening to His voice? But I want to assure you that this practice of entering into meditation will train you to focus and know the difference in distinguishing the voice of God. It is a powerful tool within the spiritual disciplines, and not only helps you focus on God, but also helps to better your life.

As you seek God in developing your prayer life, meditation should be part of your daily prayer journey. Select a scripture from the Bible and choose a verse that you can use to meditate on God's good creation.

Having one of the books or a chapter to read will help you during your meditation. I know many of you in our 21st Century prefer to use your phone for reading, but I truly invite you to go back to using a physical Bible for these exercises and preferably one that has no writings from previous note-taking.

What you are doing is allowing the Scripture to bring you into the presence of God. Spiritual Disciplines are in place to use to help us in having a closer and more direct connection with Our Heavenly Father. Practicing meditation will not only teach us how to quiet all the other voices and hear God, but I also guarantee incorporating this practice of meditation will teach you how not to Resist the Voice of God.

Reflection

The resistance I experienced when not listening to the voice of God made me feel as if I was in a tug-of-war with God. Have you ever felt like you are in a tug-of-war with God when it comes to listening to His voice?

_____

_____

_____

_____

_____

When it comes to resistance to the voice of God, have you asked yourself what steps you need to take to stop resisting Him?

_____

_____

_____

_____

_____

_____

Now that you know the importance of the Spiritual Disciplines in helping you not to resist the voice of God, how will you commit incorporating meditation into your daily devotions?

_____

_____

_____

_____

_____

If you are no longer resisting to hear God's voice, journal what God is saying to you during your meditation time with Him.

_____

_____

_____

_____

_____

Scriptures - KJV/NIV/MSG

SCRIPTURE	VERSE		
Matthew 4:4	"But He answered and said, It is written, Man shall not live by bread alone, but by every word that proceedeth out of the mouth of God."		KJV
Matthew 4:4	"Jesus answered, "It is written: 'Man shall not live on bread alone, but on every word that comes from the mouth of God.""		NIV
Matthew 4:4	"Jesus answered by quoting Deuteronomy: "It takes more than bread to stay alive. It takes a steady stream of words from God's mouth."		MSG
Joshua 1:8	"This book of the law shall not depart out of thy mouth; but thou shalt meditate therein day and night, that thou mayest observe to do according to all that is written therein: for then thou shalt make thy way prosperous, and then thou shalt have good success."		KJV
Joshua 1:8	"Keep this Book of the Law always on your lips; meditate on it day and night, so that you may be careful to do everything written in it. Then you will be prosperous and successful."		NIV
Joshua 1:8	"And don't for a minute let this Book of The Revelation be out of mind. Ponder and meditate on it day and night, making sure you practice everything written in it. Then you'll get where you're going; then you'll succeed."		MSG
Romans 8:15	"For ye have not received the spirit of bondage again to fear; but ye have received the Spirit of adoption, whereby we cry, Abba, Father."		KJV
Romans 8:15	"The Spirit you received does not make you slaves, so that you live in fear again; rather, the Spirit you received brought about your adoption to sonship. And by him we cry, "Abba, Father."		NIV
Romans 8:15	"This resurrection life you received from God is not a timid, grave-tending life. It's adventurously expectant, greeting God with a childlike "What's next, Papa?"		MSG
Hebrews 3:16	"For some, when they had heard, did provoke: howbeit not all that came out of Egypt by Moses."		KJV
Hebrews 3:16	"Who were they who heard and rebelled? Were they not all those Moses led out of Egypt?"		NIV
Hebrews 3:16	"For who were the people who turned a deaf ear? Weren't they the very ones Moses led out of Egypt?"		MSG

Scriptures - KJV/NIV/MSG

SCRIPTURE		VERSE		
Romans 9:19		"Thou wilt say then unto me, Why doth he yet find fault? For who hath resisted his will?"		KJV
Romans 9:19		"One of you will say to me: "Then why does God still blame us? For who is able to resist his will?"		NIV
Romans 9:19		"Are you going to object, "So how can God blame us for anything since he's in charge of everything? If the big decisions are already made, what say do we have in it?"		MSG

Prayer

Lord Jesus, I am grateful to be in Your presence one more time. I seek to be more like You, and to listen to Your voice teaching me to "meditate therein day and night." Jesus, in my meditation, I have learned to trust You more and more. During my quiet time with You, Lord, I want to experience You more. In my quiet time, Lord, I will hear Your voice. Help me, Lord, when I hear Your voice, not to be afraid, but to run toward You even more. Lord Jesus, help me to draw closer to You through Your Word. Allow Your Word Lord Jesus, to take foundational root in helping me not to Resist Your Voice. Lord Jesus, through Your Word and incorporated meditation, teach and guide me to be in closer relationship with You. Through the practice of meditation, I will be able to discern Your Voice from all the other voices in the world. As I continue to seek You more, I am open to listening to Your voice. I do not want to resist Your will. Lord, I pray this prayer in Your name. Let the words of my mouth and the meditation of my heart be glorified in You. In Jesus' name, I pray. Amen, amen, and amen.

Now I invite you to write your own personal covenant prayer with God, not resisting to His Voice.

Personal Prayer

Lord Jesus,

_____

_____

_____

_____

_____

_____

_____

_____

_____

_____

Chapter 3

NEGLECTING TO OBEY WHAT GOD SAYS IS DANGEROUS

Whoso despiseth the word shall be destroyed: but he that feareth the commandment shall be rewarded.
Proverbs 13:13

The Book of Proverbs is well known to be the book of wisdom. A Book which gives much credit to Solomon. Solomon is the son of David and Bathsheba. A small portion of the book is on teaching, wisdom itself, personified as a woman, invites you to grow in knowledge. The book also records the 375 proverbs Solomon follows, reflecting his name in Hebrew numerical.

We study the Word of God in order that we will have a better understanding of God's Word. The closer we are to God, the more we become like Him. This is something we truly need for our life's journey to be successful. Scriptures confirms this to the true, Our Father stated this from the beginning. Genesis 1:27 reads "So God created mankind in His Own image, in the image of God He created them; male and female He created them." (NIV). According to Proverbs 9:10; "The fear of the Lord is the beginning of wisdom, and the knowledge of the Holy One is understanding" (NKJV). Neglecting to obey what God says is dangerous, if we only seek the doctrine for truth but ignore God Himself, we will miss what He has for us. When we do not have a relationship with God, it is not possible to have true knowledge of who He is, which can hinder us from fully understanding why God created us in His Own image.

The Book of Proverbs helps to guide us in knowing the powerful and wonderful experience we can have in God, the One we can trust, obey, love, and have a deeper relationship with. As we grow, we become more open to having a deep intimate relationship with God, which will help us to develop the wisdom and skills we need to live the life God desires for us to have with Him.

The first part of Proverbs 13:13 which reads "Whoso despiseth the word shall be destroyed" is a direct judgement of God onto those who commit the horrible sins despising His Word. Knowing such danger, why would one try to despise what God has for them? Truly think about this part of the verse, allow it to take some root in your thoughts.The rest of the verse states, "he who feareth the commandment will be rewarded." Let us revisit Proverbs Chapter 9:10, I truly believe it will truly help us with the understanding of the second half of verse 13. It states, "The fear of the Lord is the beginning of wisdom, and the knowledge of the Holy One is understanding." This places us in the position that once we not only understand and obey but also respect and revere God's Word (that is the part "fears the commandments") we will receive the rewards both now and in the eternal life God promises us through His Son, Jesus Christ. So, the question I want to leave us with, as you prepare yourselves for meditation is why would you want or choose to neglect to obey what God is saying to you? Especially now that you know the danger in doing so?

Now as you prepare to meditate, below are some strategies you can follow and some items you will need to help you get into a time and space of quiet stillness.

Here are some items you can use:

- Find a quiet location
- Your bible
- Surrendering to the voice of God book
- Surrendering to the voice of God workbook where you can journal what you hear
- Soothing sounds (waterfalls, instrumentals, etc.)
- Be sure you put your phone on DND so you are not disturbed - this time is for you and your Heavenly Father
- Once settled, take a few deep breaths

If you are not used to meditating, it may feel a little awkward in the beginning but as you do it over and over, it will get easier.

The Bible encourages us to enter into meditation to spend time with Our Father. I recommend you set aside times to meditate or reflect to help you accept what God is saying. Psalm 46:10 says, "He says, "Be still, and know that I am God; I will be exalted among the nations, I will be exalted in the earth" (NIV). What you are doing is releasing everything and asking the Holy Spirit to take full control.

I now invite you into a moment of meditation, where you will spend intentional time in the presence of God.

Meditation

When God finally speaks to you and you choose not to listen, you place yourself in danger of forfeiting the promises that God has waiting for you, and of destroying the good plans that He has for you to be a blessing to the people to whom He is calling you. To avoid this, it is much better to receive than to resist. God has what is best for you, but you have to allow Him in, and accept what He is calling you to do. Rest at God's feet. Meditate and get connected to God so He can reveal what is making you uncertain and afraid. Meditation helps you focus. When you meditate, God talks to you inside your mind and helps you work through the barriers that keep you running in the other direction - away from God. Look at Jonah, for instance, he was called by God to warn the people of Ninevah of the coming destruction but did not want to do the command of God, to go to the city of Ninevah. He decided not to accept what God was saying. Neglecting to accept God's voice, he followed his own will, and because he traveled in the opposite direction, he found himself in more danger. Jonah neglected to accept what God was saying, was swallowed by a fish, and spent three days and three nights in the belly of the fish. He refused to allow God's plan to work through him, but instead opposed the plans God had spoken to him and turned in another direction. As a result, he experienced God's chastisement and was disciplined because of his actions. He also endangered others when he neglected to accept what God had said. Jonah learned the hard way, what happens when we do not accept God's directions. Eventually, he surrendered to what God said and was obedient to what God wanted of him. While our actions may not be the same as Jonah's, not listening to what God says will cause a battle that you will not win. You will miss out on the blessings God has for you and others—blessings which can only come when you yield to the ministry God is calling you to. I can't say this enough, the Bible encourages meditation. Set aside times to meditate or reflect, to help you accept what God is saying. Psalm 46:10 says, "He says, "Be still, and know that I am God; I will be exalted among the nations, I will be exalted in the earth" (NIV). Be reminded that God wants you to develop a partnership with Him and accept what He is saying to you. He does not want you to experience the consequences of knowing, but not heeding His voice.

Reflection

When I choose not to accept God, who suffers from my choice?

_____

_____

_____

_____

_____

You may be wrestling with what God is saying. In what ways can you manage those feelings to ensure that you do not neglect what God is saying and to ensure that you avoid the consequences of choosing to disregard His prompting?

_____

_____

_____

_____

_____

_____

_____

_____

_____

Why would you want or choose to neglect to obey what is saying to you even when you know the danger in doing so?

_____

_____

_____

_____

Scriptures - KJV/NIV/MSG

SCRIPTURE	VERSE		
Proverbs 3:5-6	"Trust in the Lord with all thine heart; and lean not unto thine own understanding. In all thy ways acknowledge Him, and He shall direct thy paths."		KJV
Proverbs 3:5-6	"Trust in the Lord with all your heart and lean not on your own understanding; in all your ways submit to him, and he will make your paths straight."		NIV
Proverbs 3:5-6	"Trust God from the bottom of your heart; don't try to figure out everything on your own. Listen for God's voice in everything you do, everywhere you go; he's the one who will keep you on track."		MSG
Job 33:14	"For God speaketh once, yea twice, yet man perceiveth it not."		KJV
Job 33:14	"For God does speak—now one way, now another— though no one perceives it."		NIV
Job 33:14	"God always answers, one way or another, even when people don't recognize his presence."		MSG
Hebrews 2:3	"How shall we escape, if we neglect so great salvation; which at the first began to be spoken by the Lord, and was confirmed unto us by them that heard Him."		KJV
Hebrews 2:3	"how shall we escape if we ignore so great a salvation? This salvation, which was first announced by the Lord, was confirmed to us by those who heard him."		NIV
Hebrews 2:3	"do you think we can risk neglecting this latest message, this magnificent salvation? First of all, it was delivered in person by the Master, then accurately passed on to us by those who heard it from him."		MSG
James 4:7	"Submit yourselves therefore to God. Resist the devil, and he will flee from you."		KJV
James 4:7	"Submit yourselves, then, to God. Resist the devil, and he will flee from you."		NIV
James 4:7	"So let God work his will in you. Yell a loud no to the Devil and watch him scamper."		MSG

Prayer

Father, You, are good, and Your steadfast love endures forever. I worship You always. I thank you for giving me the victory and abundant life in Jesus Christ, although I don't deserve it. You pour in to me with unconditional love and forgiveness. Father, as I learn to accept what You are saying, I want to thank You for comforting me and blessing me in the presence of my enemies. For this, Lord, I will shout for joy. Lord, I want to be in the right place not to experience the dangers in neglecting Your will. Lord, being in Your presence allows me to understand that nothing compares to You and that no weapon can stand against You. Heavenly Father, I thank You for the wisdom and the knowledge that I have learned from Your servant Solomon. The understanding of knowing Your knowledge is far more than I can imagine, but I know Father through my obedience to Your Voice that I will gain the rewards You have for my life's journey. My desire is to follow You, because in all things, I am more than a conqueror through You. Heavenly Father, I pray this prayer in Your Son's name. Let the words of my mouth and the meditations of my heart be acceptable to You. Amen, amen, and amen.

Now I invite you to write your own personal covenant prayer with God. Neglecting to obey what God says is dangerous.

Personal Prayer

Father,

_____

_____

_____

_____

_____

_____

_____

Chapter 4

LEARN TO SURRENDER TO WHAT YOU HEARD GOD SPEAK

So then faith cometh by hearing, and hearing by the word of God.
Romans 10:17

The Book of Romans is written to each and every one of us who are fully believers of Jesus Christ. You may ask why it is to those who are fully believers? Well, here is the answer and it is the only answer. If you do not fully surrender to God, how can He use you to be His Messenger? Now I am not saying you are called to be a preacher, or a pastor. That is not what I am saying, because there is only one person who can call you and He is the only one you should be surrendering to. Allow me to introduce you to Him, His name is Our Heavenly Father, Abba Father, Jehovah, King of Kings, Lord of Lords, El Shaddai, Most High, Eternal, Majestic, the One who created you and me in His Own Imagine. The One who says He knows the plans He has for you and I. Come on now, what are you still waiting on? It's time to surrender it all to Him.

Paul wrote the most wonderful, meaningful letters ever written to the believers in Rome. He was teaching and preparing Jesus' followers, appealing to them to help bring forth the gospel far and wide. Many times we get caught up worrying about possibly being called, and completely ignore the fact that we need to surrender to whom God is calling us to be and where God is sending us. Rather than be afraid of "if" we can do what we are being called to do, we should rest in the fact that God has been and will continue to prepare us for our journeys. I know right now, many of you who are reading this, are feeling the stirring deep within. There should be some feelings of emotional encounters going on inside of you right now, especially if you are on the journey of surrendering to the Voice of God, but for whatever reason, you are still holding onto something.

Romans, chapter 10 lays it out fully, directly letting us know that the only way unbelievers can be saved, is through the calling on the Lord. Simple and to the point. In order to believe there must be the Word right? So, let me ask this question right here; If God is speaking to you, telling you that He wants you to be one of His messengers to bring forth His Word to the unbelievers, why are you still waiting to surrender to Him? Romans 10:17 (NIV) says, "Consequently, faith comes from hearing the message, and the message is heard through the Word about Christ." So my brothers and my sisters what is preventing you from surrendering so that you can hear what God is speaking to you? For the Word says not to believe in Christ is to disobey God.

I pray now that you understand that God has work for all of us to do, and those who are lost and unbelievers, they cannot be saved unless they believe. Now allow the Apostle Paul to help and prepare you on how to surrender to what you heard God speak.

Now as you prepare to meditate, below are some strategies you can follow and some items you will need to help you get into a time and space of quiet stillness.

Here are some items you can use:

- Find a quiet location
- Your bible
- Surrendering to the voice of God book
- Surrendering to the voice of God workbook where you can journal what you hear
- Soothing sounds (waterfalls, instrumentals, etc.)
- Be sure you put your phone on DND so you are not disturbed - this time is for you and your Heavenly Father
- Once settled, take a few deep breaths

If you are not used to meditating, it may feel a little awkward in the beginning but as you do it over and over, it will get easier.

As you are entering into solitude with the Father, allow yourself to be separate from the many sounds around you. Having the Word speak to you, will not only bring you closer to the Word, but it will also settle you into a still moment so that you can hear what God is speaking to you. Allow the following Scripture to help you find this still place, Romans 12:2; "Do not conform to the pattern of this world but be transformed by the renewing of your mind. Then you will be able to test and approve what God's Will is - His good, pleasing and perfect Will" (NIV). What you are doing is releasing everything and asking the Holy Spirit to take full control.

I now invite you into a time of meditation; intentional time spent with God.

Meditation

Today, as you practice your spiritual disciplines, settle your mind and soul and be open to what you hear God saying. Picture yourself as Mary sitting at Jesus' feet. Although Martha needed her help, Mary knew that her greater purpose, in that moment, was to be at Jesus' feet. Allow the Holy Spirit to take you to the place where you can hear the voice of God, sharing with you all that He desires. Let go and surrender everything to Him. I would like to share with you, one of the spiritual disciplines that I became to love and a go to when I really want to hear from God. It is called "Solitude."

The Bible tells us – throughout His three (3) years of ministry, Jesus returned again and again to Solitude, where the rush of attention and the accolades of the crowds could be put into their proper perspective. Solitude is a formative place to be and hear what God is saying to us. If you find yourself crying, don't stop, our tears are a language our Father knows. Let go and enter into His presence. Solitude is a discipline that gets behind those feelings of who we are when we feel invisible and unrecognized. Solitude opens a space where we can bring our empty and compulsive selves to God. Solitude is in place to help us unmask the false self in order for us to see the important true image of who we are.

Sit at His feet. When we do that, we put ourselves in a place where God can reveal things to us. Relax, for you are with your Father who knows you best.

Reflection

Has it been challenging for you to surrender to God's voice? Explain why you think it has been a challenge.

_____

_____

_____

_____

As you practice surrendering to God's voice, what is most challenging? List the challenges. Ask God to show you how to surrender even more and how to overcome the more challenging areas.

_____

_____

_____

_____

If God is speaking to you and telling you that He wants you to be one of His messengers to bring forth His Word to the unbelievers, why are you still waiting to surrender to Him?

_____

_____

_____

So my brothers and my sisters what do you think you can do to hear more clearly from God and be more obedient to His Word?

_____

_____

_____

_____

Scriptures - KJV/NIV/MSG

SCRIPTURE	VERSE		
Luke 10:39	"And she had a sister called Mary, which also sat at Jesus' feet, and heard his word."		KJV
Luke 10:39	"She had a sister called Mary, who sat at the Lord's feet listening to what he said."		NIV
Luke 10:39	"She had a sister, Mary, who sat before the Master, hanging on every word he said."		MSG
Galatians 2:20	"I am crucified with Christ: nevertheless live; yet not I, but Christ liveth in me: and the life which I now live in the flesh I live by the faith of the Son of God, who loved me, and gave himself for me."		KJV
Galatians 2:20	"I have been crucified with Christ and I no longer live, but Christ lives in me. The life I now live in the body, I live by faith in the Son of God, who loved me and gave himself for me."		NIV
Galatians 2:20	"Christ's life showed me how, and enabled me to do it. I identified myself completely with him. Indeed, I have been crucified with Christ. My ego is no longer central. It is no longer important that I appear righteous before you or have your good opinion, and I am no longer driven to impress God. Christ lives in me. The life you see me living is not "mine," but it is lived by faith in the Son of God, who loved me and gave himself for me."		MSG
Psalms 9:10	"And they that know thy name will put their trust in thee: for thou, Lord, hast not forsaken them that seek thee."		KJV
Psalms 9:10	"Those who know your name trust in you, for you, Lord, have never forsaken those who seek you."		NIV
Psalms 9:10	"The moment you arrive, you relax; you're never sorry you knocked."		MSG
Romans 6:17	"But God be thanked, that ye were the servants of sin, but ye have obeyed from the heart that form of doctrine which was delivered you."		KJV
Romans 6:17	"But thanks be to God that, though you used to be slaves to sin, you have come to obey from your heart the pattern of teaching that has now claimed your allegiance."		NIV
Romans 6:17	"But thank God you've started listening to a new master,"		MSG

Prayer

Heavenly Father, I come to You, submitting all to You. Lord, I know the plan you have for me, and that is to give me great joy. Lord, help me get to the place where I understand how much I need You in everything I do. In the same way that Mary sat at your feet and felt such comfort, I want to experience joy and comfort with You. Teach me what it means to surrender all to You. My desire is to hear Your voice. So, Lord, I pray that as I wrestle with hearing Your voice that I will also trust You. Heavenly Father, in the times I am in Solitude with You, teach me Jesus what it is to fully surrender to hear Your Voice. Lord Jesus, I decree and declare for this breakthrough in your Name, Jesus, I pray. Let the words of my mouth and the meditation of my heart be with you always. Amen, amen, and amen.

Now I invite you to write your own personal covenant prayer with God, as you learn to surrender to what you heard God speak.

Personal Prayer

Heavenly Father,

Chapter 5

MOVE IN THE DIRECTION THAT GOD IS CALLING YOU

Shew me thy ways, O LORD; teach me thy paths.
Psalm 25:4

Psalm 25 provides a picture of a difficult journey that we cannot successfully make by ourselves. David the psalmist of this chapter is at a place and time crying out to God for wisdom as he makes decisions. David cries out to the Father that he knew that he was a sinner who did not deserve God's help. Let me pause right here for a moment, and ask this question, one I encourage you to allow the Holy Spirit to search you and assist you in answering. How many times you have been in the place where you felt that your sins were so overwhelming that you thought God would never help you? Are you ready to be as honest with God as David was? David not only cried out in prayer to God, but he asked God for insight to understand the Word.

Many times we want God to do for us, but we are not ready to trust Him in the plans He has for us. In order to move in the direction that God is calling you, we must ask for the insight to understand His Word, which will then help us to understand our path. According to 1 Samuel 12:23; "As for me, far be it from me that I should sin against the Lord by failing to pray for you. And I will teach you the way that is good and right" (NIV). The Scripture further confirms His Word to be truth, the Gospel according to John states this to be true, through Jesus' dialogue. John 15:7; "If you remain in me and my words remain in you, ask whatever you wish, and it will be done for you" (NIV).

Surrendering to God helps and prepares us to move in the direction He is calling us. Our obedience to the covenants we have with God line us up to the promises He has for us.

Now as you prepare to meditate, below are some strategies you can follow and some items you will need to help you get into a time and space of quiet stillness.

Here are some items you can use:

- **Find a quiet location**
- **Your bible**
- **Surrendering to the voice of God book**
- **Surrendering to the voice of God workbook where you can journal what you hear**
- **Soothing sounds (waterfalls, instrumentals, etc.)**
- **Be sure you put your phone on DND so you are not disturbed - this time is for you and your Heavenly Father**
- **Once settle, take a few deep breaths**

If you are not used to meditating, it may feel a little awkward in the beginning but as you do it over and over, it will get easier.

Psalm 25:5 "Guide me in your truth and teach me, for you are God my Savior, and my hope is in you all day long." What you are doing is releasing everything and asking the Holy Spirit to take full control.

I now invited you into a time of meditation, intentional time spent in God's presence.

Meditation

In our meditation today, find a quiet place, turn off all phones and televisions, and sit where your feet touch the floor. The only thing you should have around you is your Bible, and your notebook. Now, let us position ourselves to be in His presence. If you like have soothing music playing in the background, make sure it's not too loud. If it is too silent for you, have waterfall musical playing very slow. Remember, in the stillness, you want to hear God's directions and move toward Him. Now allow His Word to speak to you, use the Scripture during this time, let the Word direct you to the place. Our Father enjoys spending time with us and looks forward to us sharing time with Him. Ask Him to show you the way and teach you His path as you move in His direction for you.

Reflection

To move in the direction that God is calling you, we have to learn to trust Him with every area of our life. Are you ready to trust God with every area of my life?

_____

_____

_____

_____

God desires to have a close relationship with us. Are you ready to say, "Yes, Lord, here I am?" Specifically, what can you do to move toward what He is calling you to do?

_____

_____

_____

_____

How many times have you been in the place where you felt that your sins were so overwhelming that you thought God would never help you?

_____

_____

_____

_____

Are you ready to be as honest with God as David was?

_____

_____

_____

_____

Scriptures - KJV/NIV/MSG

SCRIPTURE	VERSE		
Psalm 32:8-9	"I will instruct thee and teach thee in the way which thou shalt go: I will guide thee with mine eye. Be ye not as the horse, or as the mule, which have no understanding: whose mouth must be held in with bit and bridle, lest they come near unto thee."		KJV
Psalm 32:8-9	"I will instruct you and teach you in the way you should go; I will counsel you with my loving eye on you. Do not be like the horse or the mule, which have no understanding but must be controlled by bit and bridle or they will not come to you."		NIV
Psalm 32:8-9	"Let me give you some good advice; I'm looking you in the eye and giving it to you straight: "Don't be ornery like a horse or mule that needs bit and bridle to stay on track."		MSG
John 16:13	"Howbeit when he, the Spirit of truth, is come, he will guide you into all truth: for he shall not speak of himself; but whatsoever he shall hear, that shall he speak: and he will shew you things to come."		KJV
John 16:13	"But when he, the Spirit of truth, comes, he will guide you into all the truth. He will not speak on his own; he will speak only what he hears, and he will tell you what is yet to come."		NIV
John 16:13	"But when the Friend comes, the Spirit of the Truth, he will take you by the hand and guide you into all the truth there is. He won't draw attention to himself, but will make sense out of what is about to happen and, indeed, out of all that I have done and said."		MSG
Psalm 16:7-8	"I will bless the LORD, who hath given me counsel: my reins also instruct me in the night seasons. I have set the LORD always before me: because he is at my right hand, I shall not be moved."		KJV
Psalm 16:7-8	"I will praise the Lord, who counsels me; even at night my heart instructs me. I keep my eyes always on the Lord. With him at my right hand, I will not be shaken."		NIV
Psalm 16:7-8	"The wise counsel God gives when I'm awake is confirmed by my sleeping heart. Day and night I'll stick with God; I've got a good thing going and I'm not letting go."		MSG
John 15:7	"If ye abide in me, and my words abide in you, ye shall ask what ye will, and it shall be done unto you."		KJV
John 15:7	"If you remain in me and my words remain in you, ask whatever you wish, and it will be done for you"		NIV

Scriptures - KJV/NIV/MSG

SCRIPTURE		VERSE		
John 15:7		"But if you make yourselves at home with me and my words are at home in you, you can be sure that whatever you ask will be listened to and acted upon."		MSG
1 Samuel 12:23		"Moreover as for me, God forbid that I should sin against the Lord in ceasing to pray for you: but I will teach you the good and the right way:"		KJV
1 Samuel 12:23		"As for me, far be it from me that I should sin against the Lord by failing to pray for you. And I will teach you the way that is good and right"		NIV
1 Samuel 12:23		"And neither will I walk off and leave you. That would be a sin against God! I'm staying right here at my post praying for you and teaching you the good and right way to live."		MSG

Prayer

Eternal Father, I thank You for seeing me as worthy to be called one of Your servants. Lord, I am grateful for Your guidance as I move toward the ministry You have called me to. I may not see myself as worthy, but Your word says, "Shew me thy ways," and Your ways are what I want to know and come into fellowship with. So, Lord, in my surrendering all to You, I am asking You, Lord Jesus, to teach me the right way. Lord, the paths can be lonely, but I have come to place my trust in You, and I know, Lord Jesus, that I am going to be okay. As I obey You, I am assured of Your love toward me. Without any shadow of a doubt, I accept and move in the direction where You are calling me. I submit to Your Will and not to my own. I pray this prayer and seal it with Your blood, in Jesus' Name. Let the words of my mouth and the meditation of my heart be acceptable in thy sight, I pray. Amen, amen, and amen.

Now I invite you to write your own personal covenant prayer with God, as you move into the direction that God is calling you.

Personal Prayer

Eternal Father,

_____

_____

_____

_____

_____

_____

_____

_____

_____

_____

Chapter 6

OBEY THE VOICE OF GOD

I delight to do thy will, O my God: yea, thy law is within my heart.
Psalm 40:8

The entire chapter of Psalm 40 tells of a celebration of God's deliverance. It's a profession of devotion to His service, followed by a prayer for relief from forthcoming dangers, involving the overthrowing of enemies. Hebrews 10:9; "Then said he, Lo, I come to do thy will, O God. He taketh away the first, that he may establish the second," tells us of a similar message to Psalm Chapter 40 specifically verse 8 which reads "I delight to do thy will, O my God: yea, thy law is within my heart." Both Books help us to understand that Christ came to make a difference. David was not afraid to pour out his heart to God, in his deepest situations, his prayer was for mercy which followed praise and dedication in doing God's Will.

David journeyed from the pit to the rock, and now he was in the sanctuary of God. His dedication never wavered when it came to the surrendering and the obeying to the Voice of God. Something that many of us struggle to do. Let me ask you this question while also encouraging you to do some soul-searching. How often do you hit hard times, and still find it hard to be obedient to what God is speaking to you? According to David, his commitment to doing God's Will and the Covenant he made unto God was because, after all that God had done for him, his best answer was to fully surrender and obedient to God's Voice. How many of us can say we are willing to be that committed? Out of all God has done, is doing and will continue to do, why is it so hard to be obedient to the voice of God?

Now as you prepare to meditate, below are some strategies you can follow and some items you will need to help you get into a time and space of quiet stillness.

Here are some items you can use:

- **Find a quiet location**
- **Your bible**
- **Surrendering to the voice of God book**
- **Surrendering to the voice of God workbook where you can journal what you hear**
- **Soothing sounds (waterfalls, instrumentals, etc.)**
- **Be sure you put your phone on DND so you are not disturbed - this time is for you and your Heavenly Father**
- **Once settled, take a few deep breaths**

If you are not used to meditating, it may feel a little awkward in the beginning but as you do it over and over, it will get easier.

God's invites us to abide in Him. The Gospel according to John, will help and prepare us to do that. John 15:4 reads "Remain in me, as I also remain in you. No branch can bear fruit by itself; it must remain in the vine. Neither can you bear fruit unless you remain in me" (NIV). What you are doing is releasing everything and asking The Holy Spirit to take full control.

I now invite you into a time of meditation where you can find comfort in the presence of God.

Meditation

What is Contemplative prayer? Contemplative prayer is a receptive posture of openness towards God. It is a way of waiting with a heart awake to God's presence and His Word. This kind of prayer intentionally trusts and rests in the presence of the Holy Spirit deep in our own spirit.

Contemplative prayer helps us as we focus on a word and repeat that word over and over in meditation practice. It helps to clear your mind of outside concerns so that the voice of God can more easily be heard. Contemplative prayer is a way to be with God, without seeking or asking for things we would like to be done in our world, our society, and in our communities. It is a time to enjoy being with God without a lot of words.

Contemplative prayer may not be the easiest thing to do, especially if you are one who loves to talk and keep moving. However, once you have this Discipline will covered, you will be able to see and feel the presence of God and being obedient to the Voice of God should no longer be challenging or as challenging. One thing we can learn from David's journey in seeking, surrendering, and obeying the Voice of God is to rest in our Father. David had to rest in God, he had to solely depend on Him to initiate communication. In order to accomplish this spiritual discipline, it requires patience.

As we obey the voice of God, this practice helps us to say yes. Saying yes is part of how we practice obedience to the voice of God. As you continue in your spiritual disciplines, remain open to the voice of God and surrender all to Him. Contemplative prayer helps us too, just like David, join God in a place of Divine rest and love.

Reflection

What is preventing you from saying yes right now?

_____

_____

_____

Saying yes to the voice of God requires us to be obedient. Psalm 40:8 says, "I delight to do thy will, O my God: yea, they law is within my heart." How far are you right now from being able to obey the will of God?

_____

_____

_____

_____

How often have you come across hard times, life's challenges, and faced opposition and still found it hard to obey God's voice?

_____

_____

_____

_____

David said after all that God has done for him, his best answer was to obey to God's Voice. How many of us can truly say this?

_____

_____

_____

Out of all God has done, is doing and continues to do, why do you believe is it still so hard for many to obey Him?

_____

_____

_____

Scriptures - KJV/NIV/MSG

SCRIPTURE	VERSE		
Deuteronomy 5:33	"Ye shall walk in all the ways which the LORD your God hath commanded you, that ye may live, and that it may be well with you, and that ye may prolong your days in the land which ye shall possess."		KJV
Deuteronomy 5:33	"Walk in obedience to all that the Lord your God has commanded you, so that you may live and prosper and prolong your days in the land that you will possess."		NIV
Deuteronomy 5:33	"Walk straight down the road God commands so that you'll have a good life and live a long time in the land that you're about to possess."		MSG
1 Corinthians 15:58	"Therefore, my beloved brethren, be ye stedfast, unmoveable, always abounding in the work of the Lord, forasmuch as ye know that your labour is not in vain in the Lord."		KJV
1 Corinthians 15:58	"Therefore, my dear brothers and sisters, stand firm. Let nothing move you. Always give yourselves fully to the work of the Lord, because you know that your labor in the Lord is not in vain."		NIV
1 Corinthians 15:58	"With all this going for us, my dear, dear friends, stand your ground. And don't hold back. Throw yourselves into the work of the Master, confident that nothing you do for him is a waste of time or effort."		MSG
Joshua 1:18	"Whosoever he be that doth rebel against thy commandment, and will not hearken unto thy words in all that thou commandest him, he shall be put to death: only be strong and of a good courage."		KJV
Joshua 1:18	"Whoever rebels against your word and does not obey it, whatever you may command them, will be put to death. Only be strong and courageous!"		NIV
Joshua 1:18	"Anyone who questions what you say and refuses to obey whatever you command him will be put to death. Strength! Courage!"		MSG
Hebrews 10:9	"Then said he, Lo, I come to do thy will, O God. He taketh away the first, that he may establish the second,"		KJV
Hebrews 10:9	"Then he said, "Here I am, I have come to do your will." He sets aside the first to establish the second."		NIV
Hebrews 10:9	"When he added, "I'm here to do it your way," he set aside the first in order to enact the new plan"		MSG

Prayer

Heavenly Father, I thank You for all of Your promises to us. Eternal Father, You said that if we walked in obedience, we would receive abundance, grace, and a full life with You, Lord Jesus. Once we are obedient, we will receive an overflow of blessings in our lives, for our children, and for generations and generations to come. Your Word says in Deuteronomy that if we obey, we will be blessed, but if we disobey, we will be cursed. Lord Jesus, help us not to be disobedient or rebel against You. Your word clearly states that when we disobey, we are rejecting everlasting life with You in the Heavenly Kingdom. Lord Jesus, please help me to have a humble spirit and to yield and surrender to Your will. Lord Jesus, thank You for these blessings. I decree and declare in my surrendering all, that my answer will be "Yes, Lord, Here I am." I am open to accepting Your will and the directions You have for me. Let the words of my mouth and the meditation of my heart be acceptable in thy sight. In Jesus' name, I pray. Amen, amen, and amen.

Now I invite you to write your own personal covenant prayer with God, as you obey the voice of God.

Personal Prayer

Heavenly Father,

_____

_____

_____

_____

_____

_____

_____

_____

_____

Chapter 7

ENCOURAGE OTHERS TO OBEY THE VOICE OF GOD

I will run the way of thy commandments, when thou shalt enlarge my heart.
Psalm 119:32

Psalm 119 the longest psalms in the Bible. This chapter tells of the vital ministry of the Word of God in the inner spiritual life of God's people. Psalm 119 overall describes how God's Word enables us to grow in holiness and handle sufferings and stresses while obeying the walk of faith. The chapter teaches us to use the Word of God in all aspects of our lives as a believer. Psalm 119:32; "I will run the way of they commandments, when thou shalt enlarge my heart," teaches us once we hold onto God's Word and trust in His promises, our Heavenly Father is able to work in His time and in His way. Our faith plays a strong part of us surrendering and obeying to the voice of God. In our own journey we have come to understand that the best way to see and be part of the promises of God is to release all to Him. Now I am encouraging you according to God's Word in Jeremiah 29:11; "For I know the plans I have for you," declares the Lord, "plans to prosper you and not to harm you, plans to give you hope and a future" (NIV).

Our testimonies of how God's Word helped us in learning to be obedient to the Voice of God is not just for us to keep to ourselves, it is for us to share our journeys and God's word with someone who may have lost hope in God and His promises. The Word gives us the power and the authority to guide someone in finding and accepting God into their own life. You may be saying I don't have the voice, or I cannot speak in public. I want you to consider something, many of us do our yearly or 6 months wellness check-up. When we enter into the room, the nurse as well as the doctor asks us many questions, and at that point, you are able to tell the nurse or the doctor all what you are experiencing. In those moments, you had a voice, and you were speaking in public, so why be afraid to share your testimony about how much God has done for you?

By sharing our testimonies God receives the glory and the praises that is due unto Him. For the Bible says, in 2 Corinthians 12:9; "But he said to me, "My grace is sufficient for you, for my power is made perfect in weakness." Therefore I will boast all the more gladly about my weaknesses, so that Christ's power may rest on me" (NIV). As well as His promises to us that, He will supply all of our needs, according to Philippians 4:19; "And my God will meet all your needs according to the riches of his glory in Christ Jesus" (NIV).

Having the Word confirms to us that God our best interest at heart and knows the plans He has for us. So now, I ask for the last time, what is stopping or preventing you from being obedient to the voice of God?

Now as you prepare to meditate, below are some strategies you can follow and some items you will need to help you get into a time and space of quiet stillness.

Here are some items you can use:

- Find a quiet location
- Your bible
- Surrendering to the voice of God book
- Surrendering to the voice of God workbook where you can journal what you hear
- Soothing sounds (waterfalls, instrumentals, etc.)
- Be sure you put your phone on DND so you are not disturbed - this time is for you and your Heavenly Father
- Once settled, take a few deep breaths

If you are not used to meditating, it may feel a little awkward in the beginning but as you do it over and over, it will get easier.

According to God's Word He knows the plans, He has for you. As you are getting settled for today's meditation, get into God's promises. Jeremiah 29:11; "For I know the plans I have for you," declares the Lord, "plans to prosper you and not to harm you, plans to give you hope and a future" (NIV). What you are doing is releasing everything and asking the Holy Spirit to take full control.

I now invite you into a time of meditation, a time I encourage you to welcome the presence with God.

Meditation

The use of spiritual disciplines will teach you to be in the presence of God and to hear His voice. Contemplative prayer is having a close spiritual union with God. Sit with God, stay in His presence, and wrestle with your calling as you seek Him daily. Paul says in 1 Corinthians 14:15, "What is it then? I will pray with the spirit, and I will pray with the understanding also: I will sing with the spirit, and I will sing with the understanding also." (KJV) God wants us to spend time with Him, and contemplative prayer will help you to do that. "Be careful for nothing; but in everything by prayer and supplication with thanksgiving let your requests be made known unto God." Philippians 4:6 (KJV) My brothers and sisters, let us trust God with our whole heart, so we can reap our full rewards.

Reflection

Think back to a time you knew God was prompting you to do something you may have thought was impossible. How did you feel? Were you open to His voice?

_____

_____

_____

_____

_____

Are you ready to be open to your calling? Be honest, and list three areas preventing you from running to God's prompting. Surrender them to God and ask Him for His guidance.

_____

_____

_____

_____

Having the Word confirms to us that God has our best interest at heart and knows the plans He has for us. Even knowing this, what is stopping or preventing you from being obedient to the voice of God?

_____

_____

_____

_____

_____

_____

_____

_____

_____

_____

Scriptures - KJV/NIV/MSG

SCRIPTURE	VERSE		
Psalm 31:1	"In thee, O LORD, do I put my trust; let me never be ashamed: deliver me in thy righteousness."		KJV
Psalm 31:1	"In you, Lord, I have taken refuge; let me never be put to shame; deliver me in your righteousness."		NIV
Psalm 31:1	"I run to you, God; I run for dear life. Don't let me down! Take me seriously this time!"		MSG
Jeremiah 29:11	"For I know the thoughts that I think toward you, saith the Lord, thoughts of peace, and not of evil, to give you an expected end."		KJV
Jeremiah 29:11	"For I know the plans I have for you," declares the Lord, "plans to prosper you and not to harm you, plans to give you hope and a future"		NIV
Jeremiah 29:11	"I know what I'm doing. I have it all planned out - plans to take care of you, not abandon you, plans to give you the future you hope for."		MSG
Psalm 141:8	"But mine eyes are unto thee, O GOD the Lord: in thee is my trust; leave not my soul destitute."		KJV
Psalm 141:8	"But my eyes are fixed on you, Sovereign Lord; in you I take refuge—do not give me over to death."		NIV
Psalm 141:8	"But God, dear Lord, I only have eyes for you. Since I've run for dear life to you, take good care of me.		MSG
2 Corinthians 12:9	"And he said unto me, My grace is sufficient for thee: for my strength is made perfect in weakness. Most gladly therefore will I rather glory in my infirmities, that the power of Christ may rest upon me."		KJV
2 Corinthians 12:9	"But he said to me, "My grace is sufficient for you, for my power is made perfect in weakness." Therefore I will boast all the more gladly about my weaknesses, so that Christ's power may rest on me"		NIV
2 Corinthians 12:9	"and then he told me, My grace is enough; it's all you need. My strength comes into its own in your weakness. Once I heard that, I was glad to let it happen. I quit focusing on the handicap and began appreciating the gift. It was a case of Christ's strength moving in on my weakness."		MSG

Scriptures - KJV/NIV/MSG

SCRIPTURE		VERSE		
Psalm 37:4-6		"Delight thyself also in the LORD; and He shall give thee the desires of thine heart. Commit thy way unto the LORD; trust also in Him; and He shall bring it to pass. And He shall bring forth thy righteousness as the light, and thy judgment as the noonday."		KJV
Psalm 37:4-6		"Take delight in the Lord, and he will give you the desires of your heart. Commit your way to the Lord; trust in him and he will do this: He will make your righteous reward shine like the dawn, your vindication like the noonday sun."		NIV
Psalm 37:4-6		"Keep company with God, get in on the best. Open up before God, keep nothing back; he'll do whatever needs to be done: He'll validate your life in the clear light of day and stamp you with approval at high noon."		MSG
Philippians 4:19		"But my God shall supply all your need according to his riches in glory by Christ Jesus."		KJV
Philippians 4:19		"And my God will meet all your needs according to the riches of his glory in Christ Jesus"		NIV
Philippians 4:19		"You can be sure that God will take care of everything you need, his generosity exceeding even yours in the glory that pours from Jesus."		MSG

Prayer

Eternal Father, I thank You for Your grace and mercy toward us. Your word says, if we delight in you Lord, You will give us the desires of our hearts. Right now, Lord, I seek You wholeheartedly, running to you, surrendering all to you. Today Lord, I am saying, "Yes Lord. Here I am." I surrender to your calling. Heavenly Father, I run to You, seeking Your guidance as I hear Your voice. Lord Jesus, I pray this prayer and I pray that I will be bound and sealed with your blood. I can easily say thank You and I am grateful for Your love and care toward me. Let the words of my mouth and the meditation of my heart find You, in Jesus' name I pray. Amen, amen, and amen.

Now I invite you to write your own personal covenant prayer with God, as you encourage others to Obey the Voice of God.

Personal Prayer

Eternal Father,

_____

_____

_____

_____

_____

_____

_____

_____

_____

_____

WE REACH THE END OF OUR JOURNEY, ONLY TO BEGIN THE TRUE ONE

Prayer of Encouragement Have not I commanded thee? Be strong and of a good courage; be not afraid, neither be thou dismayed: for the Lord thy God is with thee whithersoever thou goest.
Joshua 1:9

The Book of Joshua is known to be the book of new beginnings for the people of God. A good place to end and start your new chapter according to the plans God has for you. The book tells after forty days of God's people wandering in the wilderness. Israel claimed their inheritance and was ready to enjoy the blessings of the land God had prepared for them.

The Bible tells us that God raised up Joshua to be next in line to lead His people into the promised land. The title of this chapter "We Reach the End of our Journey, only to Begin the True One," really brings us into the journey of Moses and Joshua. Moses did all that God ordained him to do and Moses' journey came to an end after crossing the people across the Red Sea. However, the promises of God did not stop, for the Word says, God raised Joshua to begin his journey in leading God's people into the promise land. Joshua 1:9 according to the New International Version of the Bible reads, "Have I not commanded you? Be strong and courageous. Do not be afraid; do not be discouraged, for the Lord your God will be with you wherever you go". This verse serves as a reminder to us that God's commandments are still God's enablement for those who obey Him by faith. For no word from God shall be void of power, so I encourage you as you are now in place to fully surrender to the Voice of God, only to be open to accept His call and respond with a resounding, "YES!".

Jehovah—Jireh: The Lord who provides and my vision Genesis 2

Jehovah—Rapha: The Lord who heals Exodus 15:22-26

Jehovah—Nissi: The Lord our Banner Exodus 17:15

Jehovah—El-Shaddai: He supply Genesis 17:3

Jehovah—Shalom: The Lord is peace Judges 6:24

Jehovah—Shammah: The Lord is there Ezekiel 48:35

The Lord's Prayer

Our Father which art in Heaven, hallowed be thy Name.

Thy Kingdom come. Thy will be done in earth, as it is in Heaven.

Give us this day our daily bread. And forgive us our debts, as we forgive our debtors.

And lead us not into temptation, but deliver us from evil:

For thine is the Kingdom, and the power, and the glory, forever. Amen.

The Lord is My Shepherd Prayer

The Lord is my shepherd; I shall not want.

He maketh me to lie down in green pastures: he leadeth me beside the still waters.

He restoreth my soul: he leadeth me in the paths of righteousness for his name's sake.

Yea, though I walk through the valley of the shadow of death, I will fear no evil: for

thou art with me; thy rod and thy staff they comfort me.

Thou preparest a table before me in the presence of mine enemies: thou anointest my

head with oil; my cup runneth over.

Surely goodness and mercy shall follow me all the days of my life: and I will dwell in

the house of the Lord forever.

Reverend Joan L. Davis

Rev Davis loves God, loves studying His Word. She says, "Studying God's Word is such a refreshing feeling, I am drawn closer to Him more each day". Her prayer life has changed, as a prayer warrior and intercessory, she intercedes for her family and for the people of God. Rev Davis thank God for the many gifts He blessed her with, one is the gift of Faith, she walked and lived by Faith.

Her Calling:

Reverend Joan Linnette Davis, the Pastor of St. Paul AME Church in Malvern, Pennsylvania. Previously served on the ministerial staff at Mt. Zion AMEC, with her Pastor, Reverend Carlos D. Bounds who is her father in ministry. The late Reverend Kanice D. Johns was her mother in ministry.

Contact:

→

info@joanldavislifecoaching.com/ www.joanldavislifecoaching.com

51

Reverend Joan L. Davis

In May 2002, Reverend Joan graduated with an Associate Applied Science Degree from Pennsylvania Institute of Technology in Media, with a Dual Degree in Electronic Computer Technology and Mechanical Engineering Technology, graduated Magna Cum Laude. She also was the President of the Phi Theta Kappa International Honor Society – Alpha Psi Mu Chapter, and a member of the Chi Alpha Epsilon National Honor Society. She was on the Dean's List and the recipient of The Leadership Award, the Tutor Award, and the Founders Award. Her name was published in the 2002 National Women's Achievements Dean Book.
May 2018, Joan graduated with a Master of Divinity from Palmer Theological Seminary. Then completed 2 units (2018-2019) of Clinical Pastoral Education (CPE) at Thompson Jefferson University Hospital and currently serves as a Chaplain. June 2020, she was trained in Coaching4Clergy as a Life Coach.

God moved Reverend Davis from the corporate world in 2020, to become her own entrepreneur, on a Life Coaching adventure. God open another door on September 1, 2021, her business - Founder/CEO of "Joan L Davis Life Coaching LLC". As a Spiritual Director, was licensed in the State of Pennsylvania as well as the releasing of her first book, "Surrendering to the Voice of God." Both of which happens in a timeframe, that it was nothing but the movement of God.

On December 12, 2021, she received double ordination and consecration, first as an Itinerant Deacon and then as an Itinerant Elder in the African Methodist Episcopal Church, under the laying of hand from Bishop Julius H. McAllister Sr. Reverend Davis made history, as she was the first to be ordained twice during one ordination service.
September 12, 2022, entered studies for Doctorate in Ministry at Missio Theological Seminary.

At the West Mainline District Conference, on October 14, 2022, was appointed to serve as the Coordinator of Women in Ministry.

God has blessed her with five children: Noelani (28), Marlon (24), Myron (20), and twins Nathan (10), Milan (10); one grandson Nathaniel (Nate), three granddaughters Paris, Normani, and Malaya.
Joan continues to praise God for the favor He has for her.

Her two favorite scriptures are Jeremiah 1:5: "Before I formed thee in the belly I knew thee; and before thou camest forth out of the womb I sanctified thee, and I ordained thee a prophet unto the nations." and Isaiah 41:10: "Fear thou not; for I am with thee: be not dismayed; for I am thy God: I will strengthen thee; yea, I will help thee; yea, I will uphold thee with the right hand of my righteousness."

Reverend Joan L. Davis

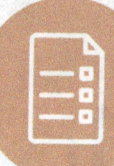

Bonus Content

Always remain grateful.
Our Father loves a grateful heart.

Prayer pages
Gratitude pages
Journal pages
and more

To find this complete journal go
the website highlighted below.

Morning

TODAY I AM THANKFUL FOR...

_____

_____

_____

_____

TODAY I AM BELIEVING GOD FOR...

_____

_____

_____

_____

TODAY I AM LOOKING FORWARD TO...

_____

_____

_____

_____

MY AFFIRMATION TODAY

_____

_____

_____

_____

Finally, brothers,

whatever is **TRUE**

whatever is **HONORABLE**

whatever is **JUST**

whatever is **PURE**

whatever is **LOVELY**

whatever is **COMMENDABLE**

if there is any **EXCELLENCE**

if there is anything

WORTHY OF PRAISE

think about these things.

PHILIPPIANS 4:8

FILL EACH DAY WITH *Gratitude*

DATE :

3 SMALL THINGS I APPRECIATE TODAY?

3 GOOD THINGS HAPPENED TODAY

TODAY'S POSTIVE AFFIRMATION

MY FAVOURITE MOMENTS OF THE DAY

Evening

TODAY I HAVE...

_____
_____
_____
_____

I AM GRATEFUL FOR...

_____
_____
_____
_____

I GO TO BED FEELING...

_____
_____
_____
_____

TOMORROW I WISH TO...

_____
_____
_____
_____

5 minutes with God

_____

_____

_____

_____

_____

_____

_____

_____

_____

_____

_____

_____

_____

Daily Prayers

"Speak those things that are not as though they are"
Romans 4:17

What are you believing God for?

- ☐ _____
- ☐ _____
- ☐ _____
- ☐ _____
- ☐ _____
- ☐ _____
- ☐ _____
- ☐ _____
- ☐ _____
- ☐ _____
- ☐ _____

SCRIPTURES

SCRIPTURES

My weekly Scripture
readings

MONDAY

TUESDAY

WEDNESDAY

THURSDAY

FRIDAY

SATURDAY

SUNDAY

S M T W T F S

Weekly Reflection

Any area you struggled in being obedient this week? if yes why?

If not, what has been helping you to be obedient?

How important is for you to be obedient to God?

Why do you think it's important that you are obedient to God?

I AM...

Today I'm grateful for...

Morning

TODAY I AM THANKFUL FOR...

_____
_____
_____
_____

TODAY I AM BELIEVING GOD FOR...

_____
_____
_____
_____

TODAY I AM LOOKING FORWARD TO...

_____
_____
_____
_____

MY AFFIRMATION TODAY

_____
_____
_____

FILL EACH DAY WITH *Gratitude*

DATE :

3 SMALL THINGS I APPRECIATE TODAY?

3 GOOD THINGS HAPPENED TODAY

TODAY'S POSTIVE AFFIRMATION

MY FAVOURITE MOMENTS OF THE DAY

Evening

TODAY I HAVE...

_____

_____

_____

_____

I AM GRATEFUL FOR...

_____

_____

_____

_____

I GO TO BED FEELING...

_____

_____

_____

_____

TOMORROW I WISH TO...

_____

_____

_____

_____

5 minutes with God

_____

_____

_____

_____

_____

_____

_____

_____

_____

_____

_____

_____

_____

_____

Daily Prayers

DATE:

"Speak those things that are not as though they are"
Romans 4:17

What are you believing God for?

_____

- [ ] --
- [ ] --
- [ ] --
- [ ] --
- [ ] --
- [ ] --
- [ ] --
- [ ] --
- [ ] --
- [ ] --
- [ ] --

SCRIPTURES

SCRIPTURES

My weekly Scripture
readings

MONDAY

TUESDAY

WEDNESDAY

THURSDAY

FRIDAY

SATURDAY

SUNDAY

S M T W T F S

Weekly Reflection

Any area you struggled in being obedient this week? if yes why?

If not, what has been helping you to be obedient?

How important is for you to be obedient to God?

Why do you think it's important that you are obedient to God?

I AM...

Today I'm grateful for...

_____
_____
_____
_____
_____
_____
_____
_____
_____
_____
_____
_____
_____
_____
_____
_____
_____
_____

Morning

TODAY I AM THANKFUL FOR...

_____

_____

_____

_____

TODAY I AM BELIEVING GOD FOR...

_____

_____

_____

_____

TODAY I AM LOOKING FORWARD TO...

_____

_____

_____

_____

MY AFFIRMATION TODAY

_____

_____

_____

_____

FILL EACH DAY WITH

DATE :

3 SMALL THINGS I APPRECIATE TODAY?

3 GOOD THINGS HAPPENED TODAY

TODAY'S POSTIVE AFFIRMATION

MY FAVOURITE MOMENTS OF THE DAY

Evening

TODAY I HAVE...

_____

_____

_____

_____

I AM GRATEFUL FOR...

_____

_____

_____

_____

I GO TO BED FEELING...

_____

_____

_____

_____

TOMORROW I WISH TO...

_____

_____

_____

_____

5 minutes with God

_____

_____

_____

_____

_____

_____

_____

_____

_____

_____

_____

_____

_____

Daily Prayers

"Speak those things that are not as though they are"
Romans 4:17

What are you believing God for?

- [ ] _____
- [ ] _____
- [ ] _____
- [ ] _____
- [ ] _____
- [ ] _____
- [ ] _____
- [ ] _____
- [ ] _____
- [ ] _____
- [ ] _____

DATE:

SCRIPTURES

SCRIPTURES

My weekly Scripture
readings

MONDAY

TUESDAY

WEDNESDAY

THURSDAY

FRIDAY

SATURDAY

SUNDAY

Weekly Reflection

Any area you struggled in being obedient this week? if yes why?

If not, what has been helping you to be obedient?

How important is for you to be obedient to God?

Why do you think it's important that you are obedient to God?

I AM...

Today I'm grateful for...

_____

_____

_____

_____

_____

_____

_____

_____

_____

_____

_____

_____

_____

_____

_____

_____

_____

_____

Morning

TODAY I AM THANKFUL FOR...

_____

_____

_____

_____

TODAY I AM BELIEVING GOD FOR...

_____

_____

_____

_____

TODAY I AM LOOKING FORWARD TO...

_____

_____

_____

_____

MY AFFIRMATION TODAY

_____

_____

_____

_____

FILL EACH DAY WITH *Gratitude*

DATE :

3 SMALL THINGS I APPRECIATE TODAY?

3 GOOD THINGS HAPPENED TODAY

TODAY'S POSTIVE AFFIRMATION

MY FAVOURITE MOMENTS OF THE DAY

Evening

TODAY I HAVE...

_____

_____

_____

_____

I AM GRATEFUL FOR...

_____

_____

_____

_____

I GO TO BED FEELING...

_____

_____

_____

_____

TOMORROW I WISH TO...

_____

_____

_____

_____

5 minutes with God

_____

_____

_____

_____

_____

_____

_____

_____

_____

_____

_____

_____

_____

Daily Prayers

"Speak those things that are not as though they are"
Romans 4:17

What are you believing God for?
_____

- [ ] --
- [ ] --
- [ ] --
- [ ] --
- [ ] --
- [ ] --
- [ ] --
- [ ] --
- [ ] --
- [ ] --
- [ ] --

DATE:

SCRIPTURES

SCRIPTURES

My weekly Scripture
readings

MONDAY

TUESDAY

WEDNESDAY

THURSDAY

FRIDAY

SATURDAY

SUNDAY

S M T W T F S

Weekly Reflection

Any area you struggled in being obedient this week? if yes why?

If not, what has been helping you to be obedient?

How important is for you to be obedient to God?

Why do you think it's important that you are obedient to God?

I AM...

Today I'm grateful for...

_____

_____

_____

_____

_____

_____

_____

_____

_____

_____

_____

_____

_____

_____

_____

_____

Morning

TODAY I AM THANKFUL FOR...

_____

_____

_____

_____

TODAY I AM BELIEVING GOD FOR...

_____

_____

_____

_____

TODAY I AM LOOKING FORWARD TO...

_____

_____

_____

_____

MY AFFIRMATION TODAY

_____

_____

_____

_____

FILL EACH DAY WITH

DATE :

3 SMALL THINGS I APPRECIATE TODAY?

3 GOOD THINGS HAPPENED TODAY

TODAY'S POSTIVE AFFIRMATION

MY FAVOURITE MOMENTS OF THE DAY

Evening

TODAY I HAVE...

_____
_____
_____
_____

I AM GRATEFUL FOR...

_____
_____
_____
_____

I GO TO BED FEELING...

_____
_____
_____
_____

TOMORROW I WISH TO...

_____
_____
_____
_____

5 minutes with God

_____

_____

_____

_____

_____

_____

_____

_____

_____

_____

_____

_____

_____

Daily Prayers

DATE:

"Speak those things that are not as though they are"
Romans 4:17

What are you believing God for?

- [ ] --------------------------------
- [ ] --------------------------------
- [ ] --------------------------------
- [ ] --------------------------------
- [ ] --------------------------------
- [ ] --------------------------------
- [ ] --------------------------------
- [ ] --------------------------------
- [ ] --------------------------------
- [ ] --------------------------------

SCRIPTURES

SCRIPTURES

My weekly Scripture
readings

MONDAY

TUESDAY

WEDNESDAY

THURSDAY

FRIDAY

SATURDAY

SUNDAY

Weekly Reflection

Any area you struggled in being obedient this week? if yes why?

If not, what has been helping you to be obedient?

How important is for you to be obedient to God?

Why do you think it's important that you are obedient to God?

I AM...

Today I'm grateful for...

Morning

TODAY I AM THANKFUL FOR...

_____

_____

_____

_____

TODAY I AM BELIEVING GOD FOR...

_____

_____

_____

_____

TODAY I AM LOOKING FORWARD TO...

_____

_____

_____

_____

MY AFFIRMATION TODAY

_____

_____

_____

_____

FILL EACH DAY WITH *Gratitude*

DATE :

3 SMALL THINGS I APPRECIATE TODAY?

3 GOOD THINGS HAPPENED TODAY

TODAY'S POSTIVE AFFIRMATION

MY FAVOURITE MOMENTS OF THE DAY

Evening

TODAY I HAVE...

_____

_____

_____

_____

I AM GRATEFUL FOR...

_____

_____

_____

_____

I GO TO BED FEELING...

_____

_____

_____

_____

TOMORROW I WISH TO...

_____

_____

_____

_____

5 minutes with God

_____

_____

_____

_____

_____

_____

_____

_____

_____

_____

_____

_____

_____

Daily Prayers

"Speak those things that are not as though they are"
Romans 4:17

What are you believing God for?

- ☐ _____
- ☐ _____
- ☐ _____
- ☐ _____
- ☐ _____
- ☐ _____
- ☐ _____
- ☐ _____
- ☐ _____
- ☐ _____
- ☐ _____

DATE:

SCRIPTURES

SCRIPTURES

My weekly Scripture
readings

MONDAY

TUESDAY

WEDNESDAY

THURSDAY

FRIDAY

SATURDAY

SUNDAY

S M T W T F S

Weekly Reflection

Any area you struggled in being obedient this week? if yes why?

If not, what has been helping you to be obedient?

How important is for you to be obedient to God?

Why do you think it's important that you are obedient to God?

I AM...

Today I'm grateful for...

_____

_____

_____

_____

_____

_____

_____

_____

_____

_____

_____

_____

_____

_____

_____

_____

Morning

TODAY I AM THANKFUL FOR...

_____
_____
_____
_____

TODAY I AM BELIEVING GOD FOR...

_____
_____
_____
_____

TODAY I AM LOOKING FORWARD TO...

_____
_____
_____
_____

MY AFFIRMATION TODAY

_____
_____
_____
_____

FILL EACH DAY WITH

DATE :

3 SMALL THINGS I APPRECIATE TODAY?

3 GOOD THINGS HAPPENED TODAY

TODAY'S POSTIVE AFFIRMATION

MY FAVOURITE MOMENTS OF THE DAY

Evening

TODAY I HAVE...

_____
_____
_____
_____

I AM GRATEFUL FOR...

_____
_____
_____
_____

I GO TO BED FEELING...

_____
_____
_____
_____

TOMORROW I WISH TO...

_____
_____
_____
_____

5 minutes with God

_____

_____

_____

_____

_____

_____

_____

_____

_____

_____

_____

_____

_____

_____

Daily Prayers

DATE:

"Speak those things that are not as though they are"
Romans 4:17

What are you believing God for?

- [ ] _____
- [ ] _____
- [ ] _____
- [ ] _____
- [ ] _____
- [ ] _____
- [ ] _____
- [ ] _____
- [ ] _____
- [ ] _____
- [ ] _____

SCRIPTURES

SCRIPTURES

My weekly Scripture
readings

MONDAY

TUESDAY

WEDNESDAY

THURSDAY

FRIDAY

SATURDAY

SUNDAY

● ● ● ● ● ● ●
S M T W T F S

Weekly Reflection

Any area you struggled in being obedient this week? if yes why?

If not, what has been helping you to be obedient?

How important is for you to be obedient to God?

Why do you think it's important that you are obedient to God?

I AM...

Today I'm grateful for...

Rev. Joan L. Davis

Motivational Speaker, Coach, Author & Group Facilitator

Reverend Joan is a highly rated motivational speaker with 8+ years of experience as a women's coach and group facilitator. Rev. Joan works with groups, individuals and organizations to amplify their authenticity and empower them to become a better version of themselves. Reverend Joan is founder of the Empowered For The Journey Toward Excellence Webinar.

SIGNATURE TOPICS

✓ Spiritual Breakthrough

✓ Women Empowerment

✓ Wellness and Self-care

✓ Managing Anxiety and Stress

✓ Being Your Authentic Self

✓ Prioritizing Mental Health in the Workplace

✓ Breathwork and Meditation

✓ Grief & Loss (Healing Process)

www.joanldavislifecoaching.com

info@joanldavislifecoaching.com

SOME OF MY COACHING PACKAGES

BREAKTHROUGH SESSION

- Goal Setting
- Preparing for an event or crucial conversation
- Dealing with indecision-making or self-sabotage
- Managing a crisis or conflict situation

MENTORSHIP

- Freedom
- Obstacles
- Reclaim Your Power

DISCIPLESHIP

- [Spiritual gifts/spiritual growth (Mind, Body, Soul)]

Please feel free to reach out for any questions.

Get in Touch!

✉ info@joanldavislifecoaching.com

🌐 www.joanldavislifecoaching.com

📞 484-882-3156